Welcome parishioners and visitors.

Merry Christmas!

After reading this book, if your heart is open in a way that propels you to take an action, please know your parish welcomes your time and talents. We have opportunities to accompany the sick and the homebound. If you're more inclined to help those who are hungry or homeless, we have outreaches for that as well. If you want to deepen your spirituality, we have workshops and presentations.

Please visit holynameofmary.org

Seeing Haloes

Seeing Haloes

Christmas Poems
to Open the Heart

John Shea

Drawings by
Mark and Franklin McMahon

LITURGICAL PRESS
Collegeville, Minnesota

www.litpress.org

1	2	3	4	5	6	7	8	9

Library of Congress Cataloging-in-Publication Data

Names: Shea, John, 1941– author. | McMahon, Mark, illustrator. | McMahon, Franklin, illustrator.

Title: Seeing haloes : Christmas poems to open the heart / John Shea ; illustrations by Mark and Franklin McMahon.

Other titles: Christmas poems to open the heart

Description: Collegeville, Minnesota : Liturgical Press, 2017. | Description based on print version record and CIP data provided by publisher; resource not viewed.

Identifiers: LCCN 2017006578 (print) | LCCN 2017029829 (ebook) | ISBN 9780814645840 (ebook) | ISBN 9780814645598

Subjects: LCSH: Christmas poetry.

Classification: LCC PS3569.H39115 (ebook) | LCC PS3569.H39115 A6 2017 (print) | DDC 811/.54—dc23

LC record available at https://lccn.loc.gov/2017006578

For Anne

Contents

Introduction

Christmas Poems to Open the Heart

A husband catches a halo dancing around his wife's body.

A man reluctantly compliments poinsettias.

A crossing guard emulates the dream-driven Joseph.

Lovers uncover the promise and fulfillment of Christmas time.

A husband and wife ingest the truth of Christmas food.

Spirits arrive unbidden.

A newborn is held on the bright night of his grandfather's shoulder.

An infant touches a statue of the baby Jesus.

A new tooth gleams at Christmas.

Everybody is invited to join the crib contingent.

Shopping drives a man into a quandary.

An old man seeks zest in youthful Christmas memories.

A five-year-old tells the birth of Jesus as it really happened.

The Angel of the Crèche asks if you will risk spiritual guidance.

The Shepherds of the Crèche ask how you articulate your
    faith.

The Sheep of the Crèche ask how you heed the testimony
    of others.

The Wise Men of the Crèche ask how you search for
    meaning.

Joseph of the Crèche asks how you make your strength
    serve love.

Mary of the Crèche asks how you treasure the gift of life.

The Father of the Child in the Manger asks how you listen
    to his Word.

A light infiltrates the darkness and fades.

Carolers from the Gospel of Luke sing to your soul.

A surprising beloved child is found in the cave of
    Christmas.

All these people and events are portrayed in the
Christmas poems of this book. The poems come from
the heart of the author and hope to open the hearts of
readers.

In spiritual traditions, "heart" means more than
the pump that pushes blood through the body. It is
an image for the deeper activity that animates what is
happening on the surface. This activity is the flowing
of Spirit into the psychological, physical, and social

dimensions of our human makeup. When we become aware of this process, Spirit manifesting itself in the flesh, we are called to behold it.

The shorthand for this experience is called "deep heart." By calling it "deep," it will not be confused with the visible functioning of the physical organ. As one image develops the "deep heart," it has two eyes: one peers into the eternal and one peers into the temporal. When both eyes are open, we are aware of the communion between the eternal and the temporal. Deep heart consciousness is holistic, holding together body and soul, spirit and flesh, the transcendent and the finite.

When we coincide with our deep heart, we know we are a profound mystery. We sense a life-giving communion with the Source of life and an interdependent connection with all people, living and dead, and all other varieties of creation. Living out of the deep heart, we see and hear the outer world as an interactive unity, revealing flows of life and love we might otherwise miss. That makes "deep heart" consciousness different from conventional consciousness, a welcome relief to seeing everything and everyone as separate and on their individual paths of flourishing and decline.

Christmas is an invitation to this deep heart consciousness, a feast and a season of these manifestations of Spirit. We honor and behold this truth by extending it into everything we think and do. We decorate our homes and ourselves, celebrate around food and drink with family and friends, receive and give gifts, participate in liturgies, listen to music, watch movies, send out cards, and loyally reenact ethnic and family traditions—all in the hope that we will become aware of Spirit uplifting flesh, of light shining in the darkness.

Of course, the foundation of this season and feast of the manifestations of Spirit is one of the core convictions of Christian faith—the Eternal Word has become flesh in Jesus of Nazareth. W. H. Auden, in *For the Time Being: A Christmas Oratorio*, drew out the implication: "Because of his visitation we no longer desire God as if [he] were lacking. Our redemption is no longer a question of pursuit but of surrender to [him] who is always and everywhere present." Both we and our world are more than we know and there are times when this more flashes forth in the familiar, when the truth of the Word becoming flesh breaks through the restrictions of our consciousness. Christmas not only celebrates these experiences. The season and feast try to facilitate them.

But one of the major obstacles to beholding the manifestations of Spirit, to dwelling, even momentarily, in deep heart consciousness, is the pace of our lives. We are too busy. During December, everyday chores escalate and seasonal obligations are added on. There is no time to slow down and invite deep heart consciousness. Besides, even if we took time, just how do we go about welcoming this different awareness? What can bring it about?

Words.

Words that come from the fleeting awareness of a deep heart and seek to communicate that awareness— humble words, broken words, overly ambitious words, words that simultaneously say too much and too little, words that betray the truth they desire to reveal, words whose real home is silence, words that laugh at what the mind thinks it knows, words that bow before what the soul intuits, words that will not look away until a situation has yielded the truth it wants to tell . . .

In short, the words of the Christmas poems you are about to read.

Seeing Haloes

Even at Christmas,
when haloes
are pre-tested by focus groups
for inclusion in mass-market campaigns,
they are hard to see.

Annie Dillard was scrutinizing
the forest floor at Pilgrim's Creek
when she looked up
and saw a tree haloed in light.

She had caught the tree at prayer,
in a moment so receptive and full
the boundaries of bark burst
and its inner fire
became available for awe.

But seeing haloes
is more than a lucky sighting.

It entails the advent skill
of sustaining attention,
the simple act,
as Dillard found out,
of looking up.

That is how haloes are seen,
by looking up into largeness,
by tucking smallness
into the folds of infinity.

I do not know this
by contemplating
shimmering trees.

Rather there was woman,
busy at Christmas table,
and I looked up
to catch a rim of radiance
etching her face,
to notice curves of light
sliding along her shape.
She out-glowed the candles.
All the noise of the room left my ears
and silence sharpened my sight.

When this happens,
I do not get overly excited.
I merely allow love to be renewed,
for that is the mission of haloes,
the reason they are given to us.

Nor do I try to freeze the frame.
Haloes suffer time,
even as they show us
what is beyond time.

But when haloes fade,
they do not abruptly vanish,
abandoning us
to the sorrow of lesser light.

They recede,
as Gabriel departed Mary,
leaving us pregnant.

How the Word Made Flesh Seeks the Salvation of All

"Who are you talking to?"

I heard my wife's voice in the next room
and was puzzled.
We were alone in the house.

"The poinsettias," she called back.

Then, appearing in the doorway,
she shared her concern.
"I'm afraid they won't know
how beautiful they are
and how much they contribute to Christmas."

Since then,
I have been uncomfortable
in the presence of our poinsettias.

When I walk by them
and do not nod
or offer a Chicago, "How ya doing?"
I wonder if they are hurt.

When I am alone with them,
I often turn on the television
to relieve the tension
of our not talking to one another.

Once
I could not take the silence any longer
and, to our mutual embarrassment,
blurted out, "For God's sake,
You're only flowers!"

But, on Christmas Eve,
after our children had gone
and I was turning off the last of the lights,
the full flush of incarnation filled me
and my eyes rested on their red and green glory.

"Good job," I said.

Christmas Coffee

I sit at Starbucks
hoping an afternoon coffee
will revive a body
that once manufactured energy
on its own.

Outside,
the thick, wet snow sticks
to the green and yellow jacket
of the crossing guard.
Children,
racing from the school building
collide into her,
hugging her waist and legs.
She is no stranger to them.
Her free arm reaches down
and squeezes them back.
Her business arm
holds on high the octagonal red stop sign.

Cars cower.
Children cross
triumphantly.

I think of Joseph.
Angels troubled his dreams
and barked orders
about the immediacy of flight.
I can see him,
grunting as he pushes off the night floor.
His free arm gathers his young wife and child.
His business arm pushes open
the door into night.
He prays for moon.

Joseph is old,
as most of the paintings attest.
The wars of life have left him leathered,
stripped away the fat of fantasy,
strengthened him for the final adventure
of protecting the future.

Christmas Time

"Under the Marshall Field clock?"

His shoulders shrugged
as if to say, "Where else?"
Default for Chicago assignations.

"Macy's clock," she smiled.
"O Yeah!"
He was no good
at keeping up with change.

"Six," she promised,
even as she moved away from him.

> The Gospel of James recounts
> that when the time had come
> for Jesus to be born,
> a frantic Joseph burst from the cave
> in search of a midwife.
>
> He found the world outside had stopped.
> People and animals were paused in place.

Fullness had arrived
and time was resting.
Then, suddenly, everything jolted forward.
The striving toward next
turned the wheel of the world
and movement was restored.

But it was too late.
Eternity had entered time.
The garden of completeness
had been planted.
Christ was born.

Arriving early,
he stood watch under the clock,
as its molasses hands moved toward six.
He saw her from a distance,
sliding in and out of the Christmas crowd,
coming toward him
like a biblical prophesy long delayed.

It was not the kiss on meeting,
or the drinks and dinner,
or even their life together since.

The fullness of time arrived
the moment they pressed the clock
into the service
of promise and fulfillment.

Spirits at Christmas

Like God,
bidden or unbidden,
spirits will arrive.
For some reason
they love Christmas.
Perhaps it is the prophesies
about the Child.

We know who they are—
	family, friends,
	anyone who ever wandered
	into the welcome of our smile.
No need to set extra places at table.
They only hunger now
for a moment of our memory.
But be assured,
their mission is not to haunt.

They will not enter in the usual way.
Do not listen for the doorbell.

Do not wait for a card.
Do not scan your e-mails.
Do not check spam.

They appear from inside,
when our minds are too exhausted
to block entry
and we have given up
fighting back tears.

Too often we push them away,
insisting over and over again,
"They are gone. They are gone."
We hug our loss to our heart.

Missing the point:
they are sent
as a hallelujah chorus
to sing us out of this narrow box
we mistake for the fullness of life.

Green River Christmas

When she was small,
her mother took her to George's Candy & Soda
    Shoppe
for a Green River Sundae—
after the doctor.

When he was small,
his mother took him to Esquire's
for a Chocolate Milk Shake—
after the dentist.

After the needle and drill,
the taste of sweetness
whispers to the body
the truth it doubts:
love trumps vulnerabilities.

The delights of Christmas table
carry the same revelation.
        Sip the epiphany of the eggnog.
        Savor the surprise of the cookie.
        Taste the secret of the cranberry.

Candles lead the way
to these manifestations.

Mothers know this wisdom.

In the temple,
Mary held out the sweet, fat baby
to the long-starved arms
of Simeon and Anna,
as the child himself,
when he came into his own,
would hold out
to every hunger and thirst
the bread and wine
of unsurpassed fullness.

My Father's Shoulder

We wager more than we know,
as the hymn says,
on bright and silent nights—
when darkness,
    although it does not yield,
surprisingly comforts us.

We take these times as tip-offs.
A heavenly peace holds us,
a Christmas calm cradles us.
If we dare,
we can surrender into sleep
and leave vigilance
to the stars.

More than once,
my mother told me,
    in a voice still worried
    by the memory of it,
how I was born with a stomach ailment.

I crunched on my father's shoulder,
my feet pulled up into a knot,
my legs unable to dangle down
the waiting bed of his chest.

For nine months,
they bundled me from doctor to doctor
until the right meds
smoothed me out.

Of course,
I remember none of this.

But it all came back
in the karma of memory
when our daughter Chrissie
slipped into my arms
her newborn Jack
and I held him,
in the holy silence beyond thought,
on the bright night of my father's shoulder.

A Christmas Touch

We received a book, *The First Christmas*,
to read to our grandson, Jack,
on his first Christmas.

Snuggled in Anne's lap,
he will feel our love
as she introduces him
to the crib characters.

Which reminds me of a time
at All Hallows outside Dublin.
At a break in the workshop,
I stepped into the courtyard.
A mother and child
were standing in front of a tall stone statue
of the Madonna and Child.
The mother lifted her daughter high.
"Touch Him, touch Him," she encouraged.
"He's a baby like you."

The baby touched the Baby,
let out a giggle-yelp,
and clapped her hands.

There was more in that touch
than I could say then
or than I can say now.

No matter
her warm hand felt cold stone.
No matter
her age of reason
was a season of tomorrows away.
No matter a photo record
would not be framed and hanged
on a wall in her house.

A Christmas touch is its own moment,
daring to reach for communion,
delighting in overcoming aloneness.

"Touch Him, Jack. Touch Him.
He's a Baby like you."

Open Invitation

The eighteenth-century Neapolitan crèche
on exhibit at the Art Institute of Chicago
captures Christmas.
It has over 200 figures,
including 41 items of food and drink.
The usual crèche suspects
are woven into the bustle of the city.
The baby Jesus gestures to the King of Naples.
The wise men are next to bartenders,
shepherds mingle with merchants,
and the sheep share pasture
with horses, cattle, chickens, dogs, and cats.
Jesus is born among people,
busy with the duties and pleasures
of the earth.

So take a lesson.
Invite company
into your crèche.

Put in a picture of Uncle Fred.
(I know he doesn't deserve it!)
Find that crystal turkey you were given
for always hosting Thanksgiving
and nuzzle it against Mary's side.
Put a photo of little Jack and baby Peter in the
    manger—
a selfie with Jesus.
St. Joseph will look better
if he is back-grounded
by that family picnic picture—
the one with little Isabel picking her nose.
The sheep, the ox, and the donkey
will welcome your pets.

Get everyone in.
Incarnation means
the sacred can surprise us
through the people and events
of our ordinary life,
a life always more than we know.

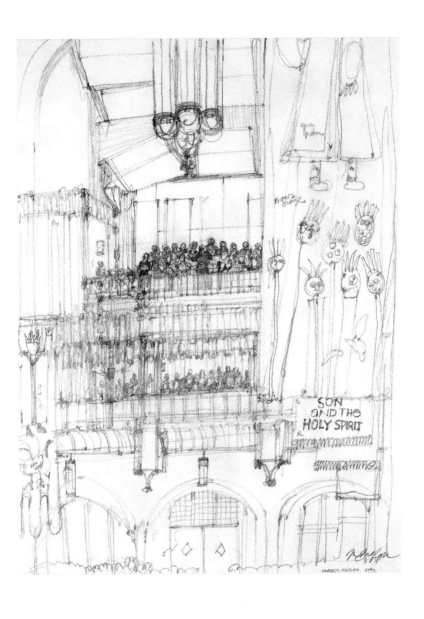

SON
and the
HOLY SPIRIT

HANDELS MESSIAH USPC

Christmas Tooth

Ever bigger baby,
months ago
we left a kiss on your squeezed eyes,
still shut from the nine months' magic;
so that
on that future, technicolor morning
when the carnival world gallivanted in
and the beautiful lady
      bareback on a horse of white
rode rings of smiles around your soul,
you would know
our love sent her.

On Thanksgiving
your pink and wrinkled fingers,
crafted in the woman's workshop of miniatures,
seized my thumb
and held me
like the string of a balloon
lest I helium into the heavens

24

to be the plaything of the winds
who, tired of tossing birds,
would welcome this weighty toy,
now weightless with joy.

Your latest trick is
a scrunch up,
a roll over,
and a yelp of surprise
to find the ceiling
where the floor was.
Brother to the turtle,
your touchdown arms go up
and mommy and daddy teammates
sweep down and swoop you up,
goalpost high.
The fans go wild.

And now a tooth!
        (Is there no bottom
        to your bag of gifts?)
It is bright as a Christmas tree,
a star in the center of your smile.
        And the mischief of your miss-nothing eyes
        tells us you suspect
it is a gleaming angel of God,
better to bite the world with.

Baby racing to boy,
today
we remember a comrade of yours
who long ago
slept through the songs of angels
and left the gifts of Kings unopened
to gurgle at life with shepherds.
He reins the stampede of our minds
and stills the hurricane of our hearts.
He is cognac against the cold
and he laughs like you.

Christmas Shopping

I don't know what to get.

Despite the hype,
catalogues are no help.
No one I know looks like anyone
who is modeling those clothes.
I shut my eyes and picture the sweater
on Aunt Gertrude,
but even in her younger days,
Aunt Gertrude could not strike a pose.
And the section on holiday home gifts—
does anyone really need a sundial?
Midway through my fourteenth catalogue,
depression sets in.

I don't know what to get.

Spiritual writers, of course, are no help.
They chide me to remember
how fortunate I am
to even have people to give to.

I should quit my materialistic worrying about
    presents
and hunker down to some real gratitude.

This higher wisdom causes me to pause,
and then I suddenly remember
the story of a man
who gave an elaborately wrapped box
which, when opened, contained nothing
but a note which read,
"This is a pause. I thought you needed it."
What if I gave "pauses" to everyone?

Of course, if I did,
next year I might not have people to give to.

I don't know what to get.

Budgetary constraints do help.
The castle in Spain is out.
So are women's purses.
Does Restoration Hardware really think
    it can compete with Ace?
I like lines like "I'm sorry, Melissa darling.
It wasn't financially feasible this year."
But putting a dollar ceiling on gifts
comes dangerously close to price tagging
    relationships.

But, then again, I think everyone would agree
Fred isn't worth more than $39.99.
Financial screening helps,
but it doesn't help enough.
No gift is got.

I don't know what to get.

If you believe the song,
Santa uses moral screening
to decide what to get.
He has a list,
checks it twice,
employs two categories—
naughty or nice.
The result—lumps of coal or boxes of candy.
The Fat Man is a genius.
But it's a path only for him.
I tried it once.
Had my list,
took a page,
topped it with a name of a loved one,
split it down the middle with a line,
one side Naughty,
one side Nice,
and wrote feverishly.
Both sides came out even.

I buy for the morally ambiguous.
Naughty or Nice
is no help.

I don't know what to get.

The little Drummer Boy—
now there was a back-to-the-wall, last minute
    decision.
"I can't think of anything so
I'll play my drum for you."
Who knows?
Empty-handed performance may be the way to go.
After all, it made the Baby Jesus smile.
But look at the competition—
gold, frankincense, and myrrh.
You call those gifts age appropriate?
The kid probably wanted the camel.

I don't know what to get.

"You know,
I wouldn't have this problem
if I didn't live in a mindless consumer culture
where people are gift greedy
and think possessions can bring happiness
and so never have enough
and strut their stuff for status."

Wow! That felt good.
Righteousness is good for the soul.
Maybe a board game where people get to give tirades.
    We'll call it Jeremiads,
a board game for young prophets, $19.95.
Maybe, if I went into the gift business,
I would know what to get.
But as it is . . .

I don't know what to get.

The people you are giving to—
your loved ones—
"Ask them," you say.
They're no help.
On one end, "Anything you get will be fine."
Why can I not believe that?
On the other end is the well-researched list
that, if you want peace at Christmas,
had better not be varied from.
But what about surprise, not knowing,
unwrapping as a real moment of revelation.

I don't know what to get.

Speaking of people you are giving to.
I bumped into one on my list at the mall.
She told me, "I have something for everyone but you.

You're really hard to buy for.
I don't know what to get."
I looked into her eyes
long enough for her to know
something important,
without any tinsel attached,
was coming her way.
"Face it," I said, "Christmas is quandary."

I don't know what to get.

One of a Kind

One of a Kind
Show and Sale Chicago
the Merchandise Mart

One of a Kind
Show and Sale Chicago
the Merchandise Mart

One of a Kind
Show and Sale Chicago
the Merchandise Mart

ONE OF A KIND SHOW

EXIT

Christmas Remembered

What boy pulled his stocking cap over his ears
(his unmessable crew cut beneath)
and found the pre-dawn Christmas snow
waiting for him?

The streetlights were city stars
guiding Magi through the supernatural night.
The boy's holy ambition was to walk the snow
without leaving tracks,
to know everything it was
but leave it unmarked.
He failed wonderfully
across one white lawn after another.
Three blocks away,
the bright Gothic God
invited him into the magic darkness
where ears were bells
and nose was pine and incense
and eyes were poinsettias and golden chalices.
As was his host's custom

he surprised him,
like a gift under the tree.
He took him up past the stained-glass saints
to the vaulted wood-carved heaven.
He told the boy he would not fall,
then dropped him into Christmas.

What man now seeks the fire of the past
to warm the coldness of his soul?

Sharon's Christmas Prayer

She was five,
sure of the facts,
and recited them
with slow solemnity,
convinced every word
was revelation. She said:

> "They were so poor
> they had only peanut butter and jelly
>   sandwiches
> to eat
> and they went a long way from home
> without getting lost.
> The lady rode a donkey,
> the man walked,
> and the baby was inside the lady.
> they had to stay in a stable
> with an ox and an ass (hee-hee)
> but the Three Rich Men found them
> because a star lighted the roof.

Shepherds came and you could
pet the sheep but not feed them.
Then the baby was borned.
And do you know who he was?"

Her quarter eyes inflated to silver dollars.

    "The baby was God."

And she jumped in the air,
whirled around, dove into the sofa,
and buried the head under the cushion
which is the only proper response
to the Good News of the Incarnation.

Crèche Characters Ask Questions

The Angel

You often position me on the roof of the stable
and that perch is perfect.
I am accustomed to sky sight,
seeing from above sees more.

So allow me to confirm your suspicion.
There is more going on in your crèche
than your earthbound squint can detect.
I am the winged reminder
to open your myopia into mystery.

Angels are many.
And you should know we show up
in more ways than you can imagine
and when you least expect.

Sometimes we appear in out-of-the-way villages
and engage in persuasive spiritual conversations
as Mary found out.

Sometimes we visit dreams
and plant plans of protection
as we did with Joseph,
who reached for his staff on awakening,
or issue night warnings and redirections
as we did with the wise men,
who bypassed Herod on their way home.

Sometimes we announce births and destinies
as the shepherds,
who watch over sheep at night,
can attest.

Yes, we sing.
But heavenly choirs are overrated
and often off-key.
We know only one song.
"Glory to God in the highest
and peace among people of good will."
Connecting God and people
is the famous dance we do
on the famous head of that famous pin.

I hope this helps you to know us.
I am sure you have guessed,
        even with these few words,
our presence raises the stakes.

The eternal is taking a hand in time.
Your crèche harbors glory.

You are probably asking,
"Why is this angel so garrulous?
Why am I being told all this?"
My only answer is:
I have been sent.
I am your Christmas gift.

Will you risk spiritual guidance?

Crèche Characters
Ask Questions

The Shepherds

With privilege comes responsibility.
And we were definitely privileged.
An announcing angel with a host of companions
told us of the birth of the Savior, Messiah, Lord,
and gave us a sign to decipher.

We would find a child
wrapped in swaddling clothes
and laid in a manger.
We hastened to Bethlehem
and found it just as it had been told to us.

Now comes the responsibility part.
It was clear
this was not a personal perk—
lucky shepherds stuff.
We were not to keep this discovery to ourselves.
We were to tell everyone.

So we did.
Everyone we told was amazed,
and we praised and gave glory to God.
No shortage of enthusiasm.
So far so good.

But deciphering signs is not our strength.
After the amazement, praise, and glory
the inevitable "What does this mean?" arrived.
We found the child,
now we needed to find the words.
The sheep were waiting to hear,
and they were not alone.
Proclamation is easier than explanation.

So the advent of stumbling words,
formulaic one moment, touching the next,
always revising, suddenly remembering,
incomplete, incomplete, incomplete!

If you ask us more,
we will say more.
If we say more,
you will ask us more.

Then you will tell others
what we have said
and they will ask you what that means.

When you tell them,
they will have quizzical looks
and tell others
and come back to you
for clarification.
Need we continue?
There's no end.

Blame the angels.
When they said,
"You will find,"
they knew it would not be
a one-time sighting.
It becomes an unwrapping over time,
uncovering layers of swaddling clothes
to reveal mysteries of love
within mysteries of love.

So welcome to the privilege
that becomes a responsibility.

How do you articulate your faith?

Crèche Characters Ask Questions

The Sheep

Most people think
the shepherds herded us along.
But they didn't.
We would have slowed them down.

Once the angel interrupted our sleep
with the birth news
the shepherds were off and running.
Revelation excites them.

But we got to the crib,
and that's the point.
We are never first,
but we eventually arrive.

But you know that.
Look how you have positioned us in the crèche.
We are on the outside, are we not?
Lost sheep, ha, ha!

We are easily mocked.
Sheep graze mindlessly,
wander aimlessly,
wait dumbly,
move reluctantly.
It is true we need
the stick and the shout of the shepherd
or we might not find our way forward.

But we are more
than we appear.
We have our place
and it is not inconsiderable.
I would like you to understand it
for we think it might resonate.

Sheep are fine with being sheep.
There are those who receive revelations
and those who benefit from revelations.
We benefit without receiving.
We are ungifted in religion.
Seeing the Son of God in babies
is for fast-running shepherds.

But we have inklings.
We feel the emptiness of the heart
—who does not?—
and entertain the hope of fullness.

So when the shepherds tell us
the hope we dare not hope for
has arrived with all we ever wanted,
we do not withhold welcome.
This is the green pasture and restful waters
of our dreams.
We quicken to the testimony
of those who have experienced
what we have only suspected.

Are sheep a portrait of anyone you know?
Unless nature or providence or luck
has lifted you out of the herd,
we are you.

How do you heed the testimony of others?

Crèche Characters Ask Questions

The Wise Men

They call us Wise Men
but we are not smart in the usual ways.
We cannot make a chair.
Our soups are regrettable.
We forget important facts.
How long, again,
can camels go without water?

Big pictures rouse us—
how all things are held together
even as they look apart,
how an unseen logic directs
apparently random events.
For us, nothing is as it seems.
Appearance is not truth.

Conjunctions, symmetries, balances
between heaven and earth
capture our detective attention.
A star moves across the sky
and we are in the saddle,
convinced the birth of the predicted
has occurred.

This fascination with deeper meaning
is how we choose our gifts.
We bring gold
    for he will bring people into their true worth.
We bring incense
    for he will reconcile people to God.
We bring myrrh
    for his death will be a path to new life.
We know who he is.
In finding him, we found ourselves.

That is why we are in your crèche.
We hope our discovery
spurs the search that lurks
beneath your surface,
beneath the practical plans
and minor achievements
that promised you more
than they were able to deliver.

The truth is the child
is waiting to be found—
if you know how to look.

How do you search for meaning?

Crèche Characters Ask Questions

Joseph

You may have me kneeling with a staff,
my eyes unwaveringly downward on the child,
a portrait of commitment and readiness.
Or I might have my hands
on the reins of a donkey,
showing my willingness to journey
to keep mother and child safe.
Or I might be standing to the side,
indicating a supportive but secondary role.
I am hard to properly place.
Wherever you put me is fine.
I know what I have to do.

I am an inheritor of dreams.
My ancient namesake
saved his people from famine
by interpreting in the day
the communications of the night.
I do the same.

My heart stays awake while my body sleeps.
I listen while the sounds of the earth are silent.
The angels of dreams only whisper commands.
"Take Mary for your wife."
"Take the mother and child and flee."
"Take the mother and child and return."

My obedience has taught me
to see through scandal.
What grows in Mary
is the work of the Spirit—
fragile, vulnerable—
pursued by the sword.
Life needs protection
until life is ready to serve.
And I protect.

That is what you need to know about me
and what you need to know about yourself.

Perhaps in your crèche
you have a figure of me
with a staff that blossoms,
flowers sprouting from the top
of the long, lean stick.
It tells my truth best.

How do you make your strength serve love?

Crèche Characters Ask Questions

Mary

I have more titles than I need.
I am the queen of this and the mother of that.
But I want to tell you
I am most at home in your crèche.
It is here,
as I contemplate my Son
I have the time
to treasure all these things in my heart.
It is here
I realize the truth of the virgin mother,
the one who conceived in the Spirit
and brought forth in the flesh.

My son will say as much.
When a roadside woman
will bless my womb and breast,
he will praise my ability
to hear the Word of God
and bring it to fulfillment.

It is what I learned from Gabriel.
He saw in me
more than I saw in myself
and troubled my ordinariness
with the announcement
of a full and unfolding grace.
I became both cooperator and observer.
The moment I said, "Yes,"
I swam in rivers
not of my own making.

How little we know!
How much we have to trust!

Hold my hand.
I will take you to the place
where the spirit rejoices,
where lowliness becomes largeness,
where all space and time is pregnant,
where the center has no circumference,
where the divine child lays his head
upon the breast of your earth.

My question is the answer I found
when I said, "Let it be!"

How do you treasure the gift of life?

Crèche Characters Ask Questions

The Child in the Manger

My Son is too young to speak.
So I will say a few words
to help you place him
at the center of your crèche
and, as you do it, allow him
to place himself in the center of you.

How many have I courted
in dreams and deserts
only to be forgotten
in the demands of day?
They put me on a throne,
so you must kneel.
They say I withhold blessings,
so you must beg.
They claim I punish,
so you must be afraid.

Then my Son came out of the water
and swallowed my word from the sky.
The dove of love descended
and my pleasure ran through him.

He never looked back,
but looked everywhere else
and saw what no one else did.

When people cried from the crowd,
he turned.
When people hid in their sins,
he forgave.
When people lost their way,
he pursued.
When people were shunned,
he reached out.
When people were in pain,
he touched.
When people did not understand,
he explained.
He gave himself away
like one who lays
in the feeding trough of the manger
as food for every hunger.

He knows Me well.

Yet no one could thin a crowd
like my Son.
His parables were mirrors.
People saw themselves
and did not like what they saw.
His actions were scandalous attacks
on the conventions of separateness.
His arguments silenced adversaries.
The cry of the child in the manger
became the voice of the prophet.

My word of mercy was never so strong,
        yet never so rejected.
My word of love was never so perseverant,
        yet never so avoided.

Of course, they came for him
with clubs and swords and lies
and he met them with Me.
I was always his welcome
for those who do not know,
drawing light from their darkness,
life from their death.
In him, I Am Who I Am.
You see,
he is Me among you.

So my question to you
will be no surprise.

How do you listen to my Word?

The Light Shines
in the Darkness

In those long-ago days of Christmas innocence
when it always snowed gently in a starry and windless
   night,
my parents would hustle my sisters and me
into the back seat of the car.
We would drive slowly, snow crunching under cold
   tires,
into the neighborhoods of the rich
to see the "lights."

Reindeer and wise men,
sleighs and shepherds,
elves and Mary,
angels and carolers,
Santa Claus and Baby Jesus
were lit up on lawns
so night passengers in slow-moving cars
could gawk through frosted windows and say,
"Look at that one!"

Once
when we returned from the "lights,"
I saw another light.
No razzle-dazzle,
no blinking on and off,
no glitz,
no "Oh, wow!"
In the window of our second-floor flat
the lit tree glowed in the surrounding darkness,
a simple contrast.
It carried me away.

I ran up the stairs
to get closer to the revelation,
only to find its moment of glory had passed.
Just a pine tree
shedding needles on the rug.

But it had done its Christmas work.
The darkness would never be the same.

Christmas Carolers

Although Shakespeare warned us
that in the season of our Savior's birth
"the bird of dawning singeth all night long,"
I was not ready.
I opened the Gospel of Luke
to do my Advent duty
and read the well-thumbed infancy narratives.
Obligation does not expect surprises.
But the songs of the first Christmas carolers
found their way inside me
and became the bird of dawning,
bringing morning revelations
to the night of my mind.

The Song of Zachary

(Luke 1:67-79)

When Zachary's weak and wrinkled voice
bubbled at the birth of his boy
and the exalted role he would play in salvation
    history,
I remembered what it took
to wring this praise and prophesy from him.

The angel Gabriel appeared to him
with the news his prayers had been answered:
his wife Elizabeth would bear a son.
But years of unanswered prayers make a man
    suspicious.
Biological laws don't bend,
and he and Elizabeth were beyond child-bearing.
Zachary was unconvinced.

Angels do not take it well
when their messages are questioned.
Gabriel reminded Zachary
that angels belong to a higher order
whose ways the children of earth
can never completely comprehend.

So the best preparation
to celebrate the birth of his son
was muteness,
a discipline that would bring him
to a deeper level of listening.

I imagine at first
Zachary stumbled into a frantic world of signs,
his eyes pleading for someone to interpret his hands
or to wait upon his slow scratches of writing.
But soon he calms,
and does no more than watch Elizabeth
become heavy with what he cannot understand.
In this space of silent contemplation,
beyond the mind's addiction to evidence,
he hears whispered words
coming from deep within him.
He descends after them
until the blurred sounds sharpen.
Then, like a long withheld fulfillment,
like a promise being kept in a way never expected,
the dawn from on high breaks through his darkness.
The tender mercy of God cradles him,
the way of peace opens before him.

He ate the fruit of silence
and his soul began to compose.

His mouth opened in a laugh that could not be heard.
He and Elizabeth were pregnant,
a child growing inside her,
a song growing inside him.
Both were born together.

How much it takes
to welcome
what we consider impossible!

The Song of Simeon

(Luke 2:29-32)

Simeon holds the child of promise in his arms
and sings that life has become so full
there is no need for more of it.
Fulfillment has arrived.
"Now you can dismiss your servant in peace"?

Try as I might,
I cannot escape envy
at these words.
How many have wanted to be able to say that,
but could not?

I think of a friend who died
while his children were still young.
At his bedside,
he was agitated and unable to talk.
I asked him
if he was worried about his wife and children.
He nodded.
I told him they would miss him, but they would be well.
He held up his hand
with the index and middle fingers crossed,
the sign for "Hope So!"
No song of Simeon for him.

We know how deep bargaining goes in us—
the parent prays to stay alive
until a child is married or a grandchild is born.
We hold out hope there will come a time
when we will be ready.
We will have partaken of a feast
that will so satisfy our hunger
no more will be needed.
Then our fist will open
and we will let go of the tight grip
we have on life.
We will surrender without regret
and lay down the burden of our days.
May it be so!

But I am not sure.
For many of us,
for me,
there may be no resolution within life,
no culmination of our efforts.
We may die unfulfilled, with work undone,
with others carrying on without us.

But if there is a chance
to make Simeon's words our last song,
we must radicalize ourselves as servants.
It is the servant who departs;
all others merely stop.
If we have given our life away,
we may know Spirit well enough
to embrace its unfolding in ourselves
and in those we love,
to trust the larger Mystery
that connects us beyond separations.

We only carry with us
what we have given away.

How living in service
opens us
to leaving in peace!

The Song of Mary

(Luke 1:46-55)

When I listen to Mary's Magnificat,
I feel she takes my hand
and leads me, looking ahead
at a path I cannot see.
Then she looks back,
checking my willingness to be led,
making sure I am not pulling back in fear.

Although she does not say so,
her smile tells me
she is happy we are traveling together
and still more—
she cannot wait to show me
our destination.

Our journey is a descent inward and downward.
We pull away from the social traffic,
from the competitions of the outer world,
from the fray whose fights define me,
from the noise that smothers
the whisperings of the spirit.

I leave reluctantly.
This is the world I know.

She closes her eyes
and I, her follower, do the same.
We enter the inner landscape of the body.
Every sensation is allowed.
Every pleasure and pain embraced.
We float in the rivers of my veins.
Then another chamber opens.
We are on the balcony of the mind,
watching the dance of thought and feeling.
Everything is moving,
and I could linger in the unfolding dramas.

But she is a step ahead,
urging me forward.
"We are almost there," she says.
"Where?" I ask.
She does not look at me.
Her pace has quickened.
"The soul," she says.

Suddenly we are in the center
where nothing is separate.
The umbilical cord to God is uncut,
and divine life flows into us,

turning our lowliness into largeness,
magnifying the life we are rejoicing in.

And everything that is
drives toward everything else that is.
We rest in holy communion.

"So this is the other side of fear," I say.
"Mercy," she says,
and the word expands,
filling space and time
until everything is pregnant.

And I know now
how we keep ourselves from this fullness—
how proud thoughts scatter us,
how riches bring us to famine,
how ruling over others keeps us from service,
how from generation to generation
we seek but cannot find
the promises that burnt in the bones
of Abraham and Sarah.

I look around.
Mary is gone.
Her work is done.

She has been called
to guide
another listener of her song.

Only the memory of her voice
keeps me aware
that with every breath
I am giving birth.

How much more we are
than we know!

Beloved Child

Mystical wisdom whispers:
the cave of Christmas,
where the child of light burns in the darkness,
is hidden in the center of the earth.

Access is not easy.
You cannot just amble to a crèche,
note the craft of the child in the manger,
and return to the noise of the season.
You may see a figurine in this way,
but you will not find the child of light.
The center of the earth is not the surface.
You must journey
and a guide is required.

Advent recommends John the Baptist.
He knows the way.
He is a lamp,
        at least that is what Jesus said,
"a burning and shining lamp,"

a torch through the darkness
to find the Light of the World.

When he was younger,
he was a desert lion,
shouting injunctions and judgments.
But after he found the cave of Christmas,
he simply tells his story.
Listen to him.

"I was not sure.
I had predicted a wrath to come;
    and when it came,
    he said, 'Let's eat!'
I had expected an ax to the root of the tree
    and instead found a gardener hoeing around it.
I dreamt of a man with a winnowing fan and a fire
    and along came a singing seed scatterer.
I urged fierce verdicts,
    and found a bridegroom on the bench.
I was not sure.

"So from my prison cave
I sent my disciples to Jesus with this question:
    'Are you the One Who Is to Come
    or should we look for another?'

He told them, 'Go tell John what you see and hear.'
So they came and told me.

> We saw a blind woman staring at her hand,
> first the palm, then the back,
> over and over again,
> twisting it like a diamond in the sun,
> weeping all the time and saying,
> 'I can see through tears! I can see through tears!'

> We saw a lame man
> bounce his granddaughter
> on his knee.

> We a saw a leper
> kiss her husband.

> We saw a deaf boy
> snap his fingers
> next to his ear
> and jump.

> We saw a dead girl
> wake and stretch
> and eat breakfast.

> The poor we saw
> were not poor.

Jesus said,
we would be blest
if these sights and sounds
did not scandalize us.

"As I listened to them,
my mind began to turn.
I was the promise, not the fulfillment.
But if you hunger and thirst in the promise,
you will welcome the One Who Is Not You
as All You Are.

"I was the cleanser of eyes but not the sight that fills
    them,
the opener of ears but not the word that thrills them.
A prophet?
Yes, and more.
Friend of the Bridegroom!

And then even more came.
It was love in the desert and I did not know it.
It was love by the river and I did not know it.
It is love in this prison cave and now I know it.
Bridegroom myself!"

The cave of Christmas
is hidden in the center of the earth.
John the Baptist is a lamp for the journey.
He will bring you,
at your own pace,
to the entrance of the cave,
to the place of his own revelation.

Once you enter,
there will be a radiance
that pushes back the darkness.
You will feel like an underwater swimmer
who has just broken the surface of the Jordan
and is breathing in words from the sky.
Notice
from whom the light is shining,
beloved child.